Pieces of me

Cassie Hearps

Presentation by *BookLeaf Publishing*

Web: www.bookleafpub.com

E-mail: info@bookleafpub.com

ISBN: 9789395755054

First edition 2022

The strength of love

1

We are blooming flowers in concrete footpaths. No matter the weight we bare, we continue to grow.

Great depths of blue

2

I don't want to swim in your eyes like every other passerby, I want to sink in them and never come back up to the surface.

La petite mort

3

Your eyes distracted me, I wasn't watching the
road.
Your soft kisses on my neck, I swerved the car.
Your hand slid between my thighs, we crashed
inevitably and both died a little that night.

I saved myself

I have never looked up to any idols.
No song has saved my life.
Not one person has pulled me out of my
darkness.
Because this has and always will be my fight, I
can't rely on anyone else.
I saved me.

A familiar face

Maybe I like the pain because I know it all to well.
It has been the only thing that has stayed with me for the longest time.

The monsters hide in plain sight

Monsters don't wear horns on their head.
They are those who we share our bed.
Monsters don't have pointed teeth or scaly skin.
They dress in our mothers clothes, they are the
friends we let in.

I will meet you there

7

I will love you in the in-between.
When the sun is done for the day.
When my head meets my pillow,
And there is nothing left to say.
I will love you with my eyes shut tight.
When my mind has left this plane.
When my heart still calls out to you,
I will met you in the valleys of my brain.

Fake smiles

You always seem to greet me with "What's on your mind?"
And I always seem to answer with the heaviest "I'm fine".

A blank stare

I gaze into space sometimes.
To see stars that aren't there.
My eyes search for distant planets,
For galaxies only found in a stare.

Words of healing

I keep my pain pressed between pages.
Maybe the words will help me heal.
Or at the least they can help to heal you.

My own creator

11

I am not shackled to any man who claims to
have made me.
The stars can't predict who I am or where I have
been.
I am not bound by a fate written before my heart
began.
I am in the front seat and I will drive wherever
my heart takes me.

I miss you

12

I could say I miss you but how can I miss
someone I've never known.
Maybe I miss the possibilities of you. All the
things you could of shown.

Time to live

13

Stop wasting time on surviving and start enjoying being alive.

To the grave we go

14

We may take different paths in life.
But we all end up at the same destination in the
end.

My reason

I may have brought you in to this world.
But you gave me a reason to stay.

Fly away

I envy birds and the freedom they carry on their wings.

Real love

You latched yourself on to me and took what you wanted, but I thought that was what love was, give all of yourself until you were empty. Then I felt what real love was and I have never felt so full.

Fading hope

The graveyard of broken dreams is growing full and I don't think I can keep disappointing my heart like this.

I owe you

I owe myself rest
Release myself form this stress
I owe myself peace
Forgive myself from these mistakes
I owe myself love
Give myself what I give to others
I owe myself time
Healing myself won't be quick
I owe myself space
Let myself be who I need to be.

I have taken so much from myself, I deserve it
back.

The brightness of you

20

The sight of him made me question all that I knew. His smile shone bright through my soul and broke apart all the darkness I never knew I had in me.

I carry my own sword

I am not a princess
I don't need to be saved
I am a fucking queen
And I will save myself

www.ingramcontent.com/pod-product-compliance
Lightning Source LLC
Chambersburg PA
CBHW070730160726
48003CB00006BA/2438